BENCHMARK BIOGRAPHIES

The Last Hawaiian Queen
LILIUOKALANI

by Paula Guzzetti

BENCHMARK BOOKS

MARSHALL CAVENDISH
NEW YORK

Benchmark Books
Marshall Cavendish Corporation
99 White Plains Road
Tarrytown, New York 10591-9001

Library of Congress Cataloging-in-Publication Data
Guzzetti, Paula
The last Hawaiian queen : Liliuokalani / by Paula Guzzetti.
p.   cm. — (Benchmark biographies)
Includes bibliographical references (p.   ) and index.
Summary: A brief biography of the last queen of Hawaii, whose love of her country led
her to write its anthem, "Aloha Oe," and to work to preserve Hawaiian customs.
ISBN 0-7614-0490-2 (lib. bdg.)
1. Liliuokalani, Queen of Hawaii, 1838–1917—Juvenile literature. 2 Queens—Hawaii—
Biography—Juvenile literature. [1. Liliuokalani, Queen of Hawaii, 1838–1917. 2. Kings,
queens, rulers, etc. 3. Hawaii—History. 4. Women—Biography.] I. Title. II. Series.
DU627.18.G89 1997   996.9'02'092—dc20   [B]   96-17308 CIP AC

Printed in Hong Kong

Photo research by Paula Guzzetti

Photo Credits
Front cover: courtesy of North Wind Picture Archives; back cover: courtesy of Queen
Liliuokalani State Archives Collection/Photo Resource Hawaii; pages 8, 13, 28, 29, 34, 39;
North Wind Picture Archives; page 11: Engraving by GRIGNION/Bishop Museum; pages 12,
41: © John Elk/Tony Stone Worldwide, Inc.; pages 15, 33, 35: The Hawaii State Archives;
page 17: © M. Schechter/Photo Resource Hawaii; page 18: Bishop Museum; page 19: ©
James Randklev/Tony Stone Worldwide, Inc.; page 20: P. Degginger/H. Armstrong Roberts;
page 24: Paul Chesley/Tony Stone Worldwide, Inc.; page 25: H.L. Chase/Bishop Museum;
page 26: Tony Stone Worldwide, Inc.; page 30: © Jeff Farnam/Photo Resource Hawaii;
page 37: © Kenneth M. Nagata/Photo Resource Hawaii; page 40: AP/World Wide Photos;
page 42: © Monte Costa/Photo Resource Hawaii

1   3   5   6   4   2

CONTENTS

Lydia's School Days   9

Lydia's Marriage and Work   16

Lydia's Beach House   22

Changes Come   27

Queen Liliuokalani   32

Remembering Liliuokalani   38

Glossary   43

To Learn More About Hawaii and Its Queen   45

Index   47

The Hawaiian Islands

N

KAUAI

NIIHAU

OAHU

Honolulu   Waikiki Beach

MOLOKAI

MAUI

LANAI

KAHOOLAWE

HAWAII
(also called
the Big Island)

HILO

Mauna Loa

Asia

North
America

Pacific Ocean

United
States

HAWAIIAN ISLANDS

South
America

Australia

Polynesian Islands

LILIUOKALANI'S STORY

Long ago, there lived a girl named Lydia. Her home was in Hawaii, where it is sunny and warm. Lydia loved her country. She loved its flowers. She loved its beaches. And she loved the Hawaiian people.

When Lydia grew up, she became Hawaii's queen. Her royal name was Liliuokalani (li-lee-uh-woh-kuh-LAH-nee). But her time on the throne was brief. Strangers in her land wanted to take away her power. They wanted to rule Hawaii in her place. Liliuokalani fought hard to save her country and her crown. This is her story.

Oahu as it looked when Lydia was a girl

LYDIA'S SCHOOL DAYS

The air was sweet with the scent of hibiscus. Four-year-old Lydia paused in her garden to take in the fragrance. She longed to linger among the beds of red and yellow blossoms. But her father was calling. It was time to gather her belongings and set off for school.

It was September of 1842. Hawaii was a free nation, ruled by a king. Lydia lived on the island of Oahu (uh-WAH-hoo), one of many islands that make up Hawaii. The school she was about to attend was also on Oahu. It was special. It was a boarding school for royal children. Lydia was special, too. She was a member of Hawaii's royal family. Her royal roots were strong and deep. Her cousin Kamehameha (kah-MAY-hah-MAY-hah) had united the Hawaiians and become their first king.

Even as a child, Lydia knew the story well.

Hundreds of years ago, Hawaii was a land without people. It was set off from its closest neighbors by the waters of the Pacific Ocean. No one even knew it was there.

One day Polynesians, who lived on islands to the south, were canoeing. They spotted the Hawaiian land. They moved closer, then went ashore. What they found pleased them greatly. The land spread out before them was lush. It was green. And it was uninhabited. They decided to stay.

Over the years, the Hawaiian settlers built homes. They planted food. They chose chiefs to rule over the separate islands. But because they never thought of themselves as one nation, they also fought over the land.

Centuries passed. In 1782 Lydia's cousin Kamehameha set out to conquer and unite the islands. This led to war.

Many were hurt; many killed. The fighting went on for a long time. In 1795 Kamehameha won the final battle. Peace came. Hawaii was unified. And Kamehameha was declared king.

After that the country was ruled by Kamehameha's sons. Kamehameha III was king during Lydia's childhood.

LYDIA'S FAMILY

But Lydia was not thinking about kings as she set off for school. She was thinking about her family. Going to boarding school meant living away from Papa Paki and Mama Konia. She loved them dearly. They were not her father and mother by birth. But they were the only parents she had ever known.

Lydia's natural parents were Chief Kapaakea (kah-pah-ah-KAY-uh) and

The early Polynesians as they might have looked in their double canoes

A statue of Kamehameha I, the first ruler of Hawaii

Chiefess Keohokalole (kay-oh-hoh-kah-LOH-lay). They had given Lydia to Paki and Konia to raise shortly after she was born. It was a Hawaiian custom to give babies away. The Hawaiian people believed that it brought different families closer together.

The Royal School was just a short distance from Lydia's home. But by the time she got there, she was homesick. The other children helped her to feel better. Soon she was happy again.

Lydia had many friends at the school. One of them was her foster sister, Bernice, who was Paki and Konia's natural daughter. Lydia's brother David was there too. He had also been given away when he was a baby, but to different parents.

Lydia studied at the Royal School until

The Royal School at the time that Lydia attended it

she was fourteen. Later she praised the school. She liked its family feeling. But she never had kind words for the school's food.

Being Hawaiian, Lydia was used to a diet of roasted pig, raw fish, mangoes, bananas, and poi. (Poi is a smooth paste made from the roots of the taro plant.) At school Lydia was served oatmeal, fresh vegetables, apple pie, and bread with molasses. Lydia found the school food tasteless and the portions too small. She begged the cook for something more to eat. She searched the garden for roots and leaves. She often went to bed hungry.

THE COOKES

The problem was that the Royal School was run by Americans. And the meals served there were American, too. The people who started the school were from New England. They were missionaries named Mr. and Mrs. Cooke. They had come to Hawaii to teach Hawaiian children American ways.

It wasn't just the food the Cookes changed. They also changed the way the children dressed. Bare feet were part of the easy Hawaiian lifestyle. The Cookes made the children wear shoes. Scant clothing kept Hawaiians cool in the warm sunshine. The Cookes made the children cover up. Hawaiians liked to hang flower chains, called leis, around their necks. The Cookes told the children that flowers belonged in gardens.

Most of all, the Cookes tried to change the children's religious beliefs. They taught them Christian ideas about good

Lydia as a teenager

and evil. They made them pray to one god instead of many.

Missionaries like the Cookes meant well. But many Hawaiians did not like them. They did not like the changes the missionaries brought to Hawaii.

Even though the Royal School had many rules, it was still a good school. Lydia learned English there, which she used later as queen. She studied music, and became a noted singer and song-writer when she grew up. And the Christian beliefs she was taught became part of her life.

The Royal School closed in the early 1850s, and Lydia finished her education at a day school.

LYDIA'S MARRIAGE AND WORK

At the age of sixteen, with her schooling behind her, Lydia began to think about marriage. She remembered a boy from the past. She had liked him. He was an American named John Dominis. He had been a student at the school next to hers. Sometimes Lydia had spoken to him over the wall that separated the two schools. Then she and John had lost touch.

Lydia and John met again in 1854. John was now a general in the Hawaiian army and a friend of the new king, Kamehameha IV. Lydia was also the king's friend. She and John spent many hours together and soon fell in love. They married in 1862. Lydia moved into Washington Place, the Hawaiian home of John's family.

John was a kind and loving husband. He was also a friend to the Hawaiian nation. He worked as an adviser to the King. In 1863 he was made governor of Oahu. Lydia was thrilled and proud. She often went with him on his trips around the island to meet the people.

Washington Place today

John Dominis around the time of his marriage to Lydia

Lydia loved being with John. But she also knew that she needed work of her own.

GOOD DEEDS

Lydia decided to do as much as she could to help the Hawaiian people. When her foster parents died in the mid-1850s, they left her money. She used it to start a school for orphaned children. She also spoke out about the importance of education for girls. And whenever she could, she traveled throughout the islands to help Hawaiians in need.

In 1876 she went to the island of Molokai (mahl-uh-KYE), home to Hawaiians who had leprosy. Leprosy is a frightening disease. People believed that it was easily spread. But Lydia wasn't afraid. She walked among the lepers

A view from the beautiful island of Oahu. Lydia's husband was named governor of Oahu shortly after they were married.

Mauna Loa during one of its eruptions

giving out gifts of books, clothing, and food. The people loved her for her courage and kindness.

In 1881 Lydia visited the city of Hilo (HEE-loh) on the Big Island. Hilo is close to the biggest volcano in the world, Mauna Loa (mow-nuh LOW-uh). Mauna Loa had erupted many times in its long history. It seemed about to erupt again.

The people were worried. They knew their homes and very lives were at risk. Lydia walked through the streets trying to comfort the people. She brought along the Royal Hawaiian Band to play. She believed that music and her encouraging words would lift the people's spirits. She was right.

And to everyone's relief, Mauna Loa did not erupt that time.

LYDIA'S BEACH HOUSE

Lydia loved her work. But she also liked to have fun. In the mid-1860s she had a vacation home built for herself. It was on Waikiki Beach along the Pacific Ocean. From its big porch she could look out over the sand and the sea. She spent days at a time there. She sang. She played the piano. She strummed her guitar. And she wrote songs.

"To compose was as natural to me as to breathe," she said. In one week's time she wrote a national anthem for Hawaii. Later she wrote "Aloha Oe," which means "Farewell to Thee." The song was translated into English. The sad words and sweet melody of its chorus have helped make it one of the most famous Hawaiian songs ever written.

Farewell to thee, farewell to thee,
Thou charming one who dwells in shaded bowers.
One fond embrace e'er I depart,
Until we meet again.

Lydia also had outdoor parties called luaus (LOO-ow) at her beach house. Guests at luaus eat specially prepared

Sheet music for "Aloha Oe"

A modern-day hula dancer

Hawaiian foods: pig roasted over huge bonfires, chicken stewed in coconut milk, fish, mangoes, sugarcane, pineapple, and poi.

After the meal, there is singing. Dancers do the hula. The hula is a Hawaiian dance that tells a story using movements of the arms and hands.

LYDIA'S SPECIAL LUAU

One spring day in 1869 Lydia had a very special luau. It was in honor of a visitor from England. The son of Queen Victoria had come. Lydia invited many important Hawaiians to the luau to meet him. Her foster sister, Bernice, was there. Her brother David was there. And King

Kamehameha V was there, too. The luau was a great success. It brought the English and Hawaiian people closer together. Lydia was pleased. But she wasn't surprised. She knew that everyone loved luaus.

Lydia's foster sister, Bernice

Hawaii's great beauty attracted more and more American businessmen.

CHANGES COME

Time passed. Lydia began to see changes in her country. More and more Americans were coming to stay. And now they were not just missionaries.

By the early 1870s American bankers and lawyers were also arriving. They were drawn to Hawaii by its beauty and promise. They liked its warm climate and lush plant life. They liked its blue harbors and sandy beaches. They saw its growing cities as good places to live and do business. Lydia feared that they would soon take over the land. She worried that Hawaiian customs would fade away.

Lydia was right to worry. Many of the American settlers began to buy up Hawaiian land. They hired workers from China and Japan to farm it. They used the land to grow sugarcane. When their crops ripened, they shipped them around the world. The American settlers became rich and powerful.

Soon the Americans tried to become part of the Hawaiian government. Some

King Kalakaua, Lydia's brother

even wanted Hawaii to become part of the United States. And without meaning to, it was Lydia's brother David who helped make that happen.

THE AMERICAN TREATY

In 1874 David was crowned King Kalakaua(kah-LAH-KAH-ew-uh). He wanted Hawaii and the United States to be friends. He traveled to Washington, D.C., to meet with President Ulysses Grant.

The king and the president drew up a treaty about the American sugar growers in Hawaii. The treaty said that the sugar growers could ship their sugar to the United States without paying American taxes. The treaty also said that only Americans could use Hawaii's harbors.

The treaty was good for the Americans. It meant that they could keep more

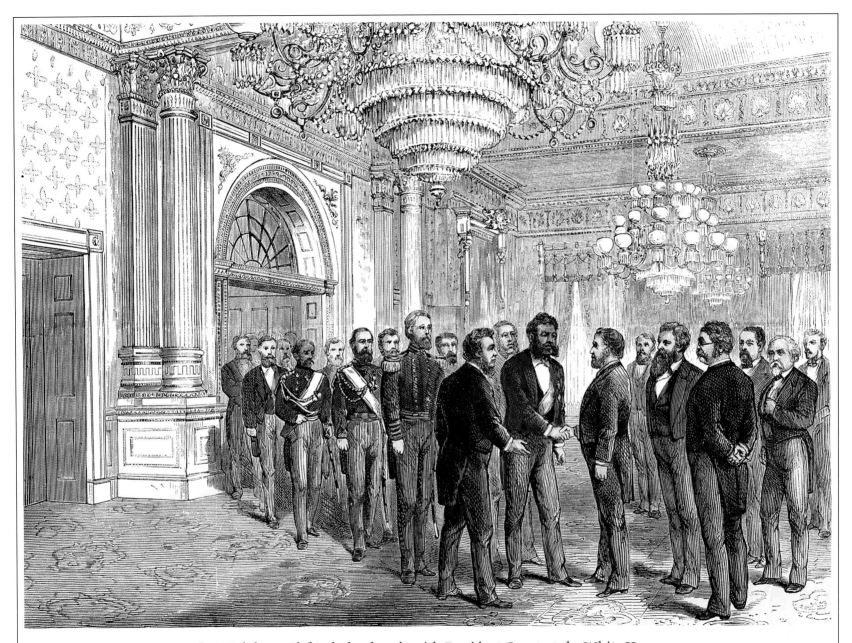

King Kalakaua (left) shakes hands with President Grant at the White House.
John Dominis, wearing a blue uniform, stands behind the king.

Iolani Palace

of the money they earned. It also shut other nations out of the sugar market. The Americans in Hawaii became even richer than they had been before.

But the treaty was not good for the Hawaiians. It did nothing to help them. Even the new jobs it created continued to go to workers from China and Japan.

Some Hawaiians spoke out against the treaty and the king. Even Lydia was upset. She loved David, but she worried about what he had done.

TROUBLE COMES
In 1887 Lydia went to Washington, D.C. She met with the new president of the United States, Grover Cleveland. She told him that American landowners were taking over Hawaii. She feared for Hawaii's freedom.

The president understood Lydia's concern. He told her that he, too, wanted Hawaii to remain free. Lydia felt better. She believed that her visit had helped.

But before Lydia returned home, something terrible happened. A group of American businessmen marched on Iolani (eye-oh-LAH-nee) Palace, where King Kalakaua lived. They had guns. They threatened the king. They forced him to sign a new constitution that gave Americans in Hawaii the right to make Hawaii's laws.

With the stroke of his royal pen, the king signed away his powers. From then on he was just a figurehead.

Four years after the constitution was signed, King Kalakaua died. Lydia believed that it was grief over his own deeds that killed him.

QUEEN LILIUOKALANI

On January 29, 1891, Lydia was crowned Queen Liliuokalani. But she knew that she was a queen in name only. She must fight the American takeover. She must get back her royal powers. And above all, she must return Hawaii to the Hawaiian people.

Liliuokalani began her reign by demanding that the American lawmakers give up power. They refused. She wrote a new constitution giving herself the right to rule. This angered the Americans, and they planned her overthrow.

They tried to get the Hawaiian people to turn against her. The Americans told the Hawaiians that Liliuokalani was spending government money on herself.

The Hawaiians knew and trusted their queen and did not believe the lie. Many were ready to fight for Liliuokalani, but she begged them not to. She told them that no blood must be shed. She wanted change through peaceful means. She warned that there must not be war.

But Liliuokalani's enemies were not to be stilled. With the help of American

Lydia on the day she became queen

marines, they forced the queen from the throne. Faced with soldiers and guns, she had no choice but to step down.

THE REPUBLIC OF HAWAII

On January 17, 1893, an American named Sanford Dole took over as Hawaii's leader. Once again, Liliuokalani asked President Cleveland for help. The president still believed that Hawaii should be ruled by the queen. He tried to get Dole to give up power, but Dole refused.

On July 4, 1894, Sanford Dole declared Hawaii a republic and became its president. Liliuokalani was told to leave Iolani Palace. She went back to her home at Washington Place.

Liliuokalani was sad. She had lost her country. She had lost her crown. She had

Sanford Dole

no one to turn to for comfort or help. Both her foster sister, Bernice, and her husband, John, had died. John's death was especially hard for her. He had been her closest adviser and friend.

Liliuokalani's followers still wanted the queen to be restored to her throne. In 1895 they tried to overthrow the republic. They failed. Many of them were captured and jailed.

ARREST AND IMPRISONMENT

Dole's government blamed Liliuokalani for the uprising. They arrested her for treason, and imprisoned her in the royal palace. She was locked in an upstairs apartment. A guard was placed at her door. No longer a queen, she was now not even free.

"That first night of my imprisonment

Queen Liliuokalani being taken prisoner

was the longest night I have ever passed in my life," she later said.

Liliuokalani was forced to admit to crimes she had not committed. She was made to sign a paper giving up her right to the throne. She was told that if she did not sign it, her loyal followers would be shot.

Liliuokalani was tried and sentenced to five years of labor and a fine of five thousand dollars. Sanford Dole, however, thought the sentence was too harsh, and it was never carried out. She remained a prisoner in Iolani Palace for eight months.

FRESH FLOWERS

Soon the government saw that Liliuokalani was no threat. They gave her back many of her freedoms. She was allowed to write. She was allowed to play her instruments. And she was permitted to compose music.

The Hawaiian people did not forget their queen during the time that she was shut away. Every day they brought bouquets of fresh flowers to the palace doors. Soon she was permitted to receive the bouquets.

FREEDOM

Liliuokalani was released from Iolani Palace in September of 1895. She returned to Washington Place.

Heartsick and bitter, she left Hawaii in December of 1896. She spent about eight months in the United States. She visited friends in San Francisco and Boston. She met with government leaders in Washington, D.C. She also called

Yellow hibiscus, one of Liliuokalani's favorite flowers. One day it would be Hawaii's state flower.

on President Cleveland at the White House. She asked again that Hawaii be given its freedom. The president still wanted that, too. But it wasn't to be.

REMEMBERING LILIUOKALANI

In 1897 a new American president, William McKinley, took office. A year later he signed a paper annexing Hawaii to the United States. Two years after that Hawaii became a United States territory. Sanford Dole became its governor.

Liliuokalani's visit to the United States had not saved her country. But it had helped to make her feel better. While she was in the United States, she published a collection of her songs. She also wrote her autobiography. She called it *Hawaii's Story by Hawaii's Queen*.

Liliuokalani returned to Hawaii in the summer of 1897. Many important people came to see her at Washington Place. World leaders visited her. And personal friends came, too. Washington Place was lively and happy.

As the years passed, Liliuokalani watched a new Hawaii emerge. Americans were everywhere. Liliuokalani realized that she could not stop the changes in her homeland. But she found it hard to accept them.

The turning point for Liliuokalani

came in 1917. The world was at war. Nations were fighting nations in a series of cruel and bloody battles. The United States entered the war in April. Hawaiians were part of the American forces. When five Hawaiian sailors died in battle, Liliuokalani was stirred. Feelings of patriotism welled up inside her. But they were not for Hawaii. They were for the United States of America.

A NEW FLAG

In a show of support for America's troops, Liliuokalani had the Hawaiian flag over Washington Place lowered. She watched with pride as the American flag was raised up in its place.

Liliuokalani died shortly afterward. She was seventy-nine.

Five years after Liliuokalani's death,

Hawaiian residents receiving news of Hawaii's annexation to the United States

A Hawaiian newsboy selling copies of the first papers announcing statehood

Washington Place was taken over by the government. It has served as the home of Hawaii's governors ever since.

Iolani Palace still stands. It is the only palace on American soil. It was used as a government building until 1969. After that it was restored to its royal splendor. It is now a museum open to the public.

In 1959 Hawaii became America's fiftieth state. Since that time it has been an important member of the American family. It sends senators and representatives to the United States Congress. It follows the laws of the United States under the United States president.

Much has happened to Hawaii in the years since Liliuokalani's death. But the Hawaiian people still have not forgotten their queen. A thirty-acre park in Hilo is dedicated to her. It is called Liliuokalani

Liliuokalani Gardens, the park built in honor of the last Hawaiian queen

The statue of Queen Liliuokalani outside Iolani Palace. Every day, it is draped with fresh flowers.

Gardens. It blooms year-round with the flowers she loved. And a larger-than-life-size bronze statue of her stands outside Iolani Palace. It is decorated each day with chains of fresh blossoms.

History may now remember her as the monarch who lost the throne. But to the Hawaiian people, Liliuokalani will always be queen.

Glossary

adviser: a person who offers ideas or advice, in order to help another person

annex: to add land

autobiography: the story of a person's life written by that person

Congress: the group of people who make the laws of the United States

conquer: to win control over land or people through war

constitution: a paper stating the laws and plan of government of a nation

figurehead: a king or queen with no power

government: the people and laws that make a country run

governor: the person in charge of the government of a state or territory

island: land surrounded by water

missionary: a person who travels to teach his or her religious beliefs to others

patriotism: love for one's country

GLOSSARY

representative: a member of the United States Congress who serves in the House of Representatives, one of two bodies that make the country's laws

republic: a country whose leaders are chosen by the people

senator: a member of the United States Congress who serves in the Senate, one of two bodies that make the country's laws

tax: money paid to a government

territory: land that is under the control of a distant country

treason: acting against one's country by helping an enemy

treaty: an agreement between countries

uninhabited: having no people

unite: to bring together as one

To Learn More About Hawaii and Its Queen

About Queen Liliuokalani

Liliuokalani by Mary Malone
published by Garrard Publishing Company, 1975.
The facts and events of Liliuokalani's life are presented through narration and invented dialogue.
Reading level: primary grades

Last Queen of Hawaii: Liliuokalani by Hazel Wilson
published by Alfred A. Knopf, 1963.
This book provides a detailed account of Liliuokalani's life and reign.
Reading level: middle grades

Notable American Women, 1607–1950: A Biographical Dictionary
published by Harvard University Press, 1971.
The Liliuokalani entry on pages 403 and 404 of Volume II outlines the basic facts of the queen's life and reign.
Reading level: young adult

Hawaii's Story by Hawaii's Queen by Liliuokalani
published by Charles E. Tuttle Company, 1964.
This is Liliuokalani's life story in her own words.
Reading level: adult

Betrayal
produced by the Kukui Foundation and
Hawaii Public Television, 1993.
In this videotape, actors recreate the story
of Liliuokalani's overthrow.
Viewing level: all ages

About Hawaii

From Sea to Shining Sea: Hawaii by Dennis
Brindell Fradin
published by Childrens Press, 1994.
Hawaii's history, geography, and way of
life are covered through simple text and
photographs.
Reading level: primary grades

America the Beautiful: Hawaii by Sylvia
McNair

published by Childrens Press, 1990.
This book gives a detailed account of many
facets of Hawaiian culture.
Reading level: middle grades

Insight Guides: Hawaii
published by Houghton Mifflin, 1994.
This travel guide presents information on
all aspects of Hawaiian history and life.
Reading level: adult

Forever Hawaii: A Video Portrait by John and
Sheila Dobovan
produced by Video Releasing Company,
1985.
This videotape provides a visual and narra-
tive tour of the major Hawaiian islands.
Viewing level: all ages

Index

Page numbers for illustrations are in boldface

Aloha Oe, 22, **23**
America
    American flag, 39
    American military, 32-33
    American settlers in Hawaii,
       27-28
    American Treaty, 28-31
    Americans at Royal School,
       14-15

Bernice (foster sister), 12, 24,
    25, 34

China, sugar growers from, 27,
    31
Cleveland, Grover, 31, 33, 37
Cooke, Mr. and Mrs., 14-15

Dole, Sanford, 33, **34**, 36, 38
Dominis, John, 16, **18**, 19, **29**, 34

flag, Hawaiian and American, 39
food, Hawaiian, 14

luaus, 22, 24-25

Grant, Ulysses S., 28, **29**

Hawaii, 9-10, **26**
    annexation of, 38, **39**
    republic of, 33-34
    statehood, **40**
Hawaii's Story by Hawaii's Queen,
    38
Hilo, 21, 40-42
hula, **24**

Iolani Palace, **30**, 31, 33, 36, 40,
    42

Japan, sugar growers from, 27,
    31

Kalakaua, King (David), 12, 24,
    28, **29**, 31
Kamehameha I (The Great), 9,
    10, **12**

Kamehameha III, 10
Kamehameha IV, 16
Kamehameha V, 25
Kapaakea, Chief, 10, 12
Keohokalole, Chiefess, 12
Konia, 10, 12

leis (flower chains), 14
leprosy, 18, 21
Liliuokalani Gardens, 40, **41**-42
Liliuokalani, Queen (Lydia)
    Aloha Oe, 22, **23**
    arrest and imprisonment, 34,
       35-36
    beach house, 22-26
    becomes queen, 32, **33**
    childhood and school days,
       9-15
    Christian beliefs, 14, 15
    death, 39-40
    family, 10, 12-14
    freedom, 36-37
    at leper settlement, 18, 21

marriage to General Dominis, 16
national anthem, 22
Republic of Hawaii, 33-34
school for orphans, 18
songwriting, 22, 36, 38
statue of, **42**
as a teenager, **15**
visits to Washington, D.C., 31, 36-37
luaus, 22, 24-25

McKinley, William, 38
Mauna Loa, **20**, 21
missionaries, 14, 15
Molokai, 18
music, 21, 22, 36, 38

Oahu, **8**, 9, 10, 16, **19**

Paki, 10, 12
poi, 14
Polynesians, 10, **11**

Royal Hawaiian Band, 21
Royal School, 12, **13**, 14-15

sugar growers, 27, 28

volcanoes, **20**, 21

Waikiki Beach, 22
Washington Place, 16, **17**, 33, 36, 38, 39, 40

PAULA GUZZETTI spent the first part of her professional life teaching grades kindergarten through eight. Now a full-time writer, she has a special interest in history, literature, and the arts. In addition to *The Last Hawaiian Queen*, Paula's books for children include *A Family Called Brontë, The White House*, and *Jim Carrey*, a biography of the comic actor. Paula lives in Philadelphia and enjoys the city's many gardens and parks.